DATE DUE

GREAT AMERICAN
HORSES
AN IMAGINATION LIBRARY SERIES

MORGANS

by Victor Gentle and Janet Perry

Gareth Stevens Publishing
MILWAUKEE

For a free color catalog describing Gareth Stevens' list of high-quality books and multimedia programs, call 1-800-542-2595 (USA) or 1-800-461-9120 (Canada). Gareth Stevens Publishing's Fax: (414) 225-0377.
See our catalog, too, on the World Wide Web: gsinc.com

Library of Congress Cataloging-in-Publication Data

Gentle, Victor.
    Morgans / by Victor Gentle and Janet Perry.
       p. cm. — (Great American horses: an imagination library series)
    Includes bibliographical references (p. 23) and index.
    Summary: Describes the physical features and other characteristics of the first original American horse breed.
    ISBN 0-8368-2130-0 (lib. bdg.)
    1. Morgan horse—Juvenile literature. [1. Morgan horse. 2. Horses.]
I. Perry, Janet, 1960- . II. Title. III. Series: Gentle, Victor. Great American horses.
SF293.M8G45   1998
636.1'77—dc21   98-14796

First published in 1998 by
Gareth Stevens Publishing
1555 North RiverCenter Drive, Suite 201
Milwaukee, WI 53212 USA

Text: Victor Gentle and Janet Perry
Page layout: Victor Gentle, Janet Perry, and Renee M. Bach
Cover design: Renee M. Bach
Series editor: Patricia Lantier-Sampon
Editorial assistants: Mary Dykstra and Diane Laska

Photo credits: Cover, pp. 5, 7, 9, 11, 13, 15, 19, 21, and 22 © Bob Langrish; p. 17 © Culver Pictures

Printed in the United States of America

1 2 3 4 5 6 7 8 9 02 01 00 99 98

Front cover: With head held proudly and tail streaming in the wind, this **bay** Morgan shines with the spirit that has made Morgans famous.

TABLE OF CONTENTS

Words that appear in the glossary are printed in **boldface**
type the first time they occur in the text.

A NEW BREED OF AMERICAN

In the Old World of Europe, people used different **breeds** of horses for different jobs. But settlers in the New World had very little money and needed horses that could do many tasks, such as pull plows, carry heavy loads, and carry people from place to place. Owners also wanted beautiful horses.

So, the settlers created their own horse breeds. A breed is a group of horses that has been carefully **bred** by people for certain features. When a horse is bred, a person selects a mare (a female horse) and a stallion (a male horse) to **mate** and have foals (baby horses). Hopefully, the foals will have their parents' features. The Morgan horse breed happened this way; it was the first original American breed.

A good example of power with attitude, the beauty of this stallion hides a tough interior. What a tail he has! It's as amazing as the tale of how Morgans came to be.

JUSTIN MORGAN'S LUCKY DAY

Justin Morgan lived from 1747 to 1798 in New England. He was a gentle man who lived a quiet life. He loved music, and he taught it for a living. But he did not earn much money. One day, he had to walk a long way to a student's farm to collect his pay for music lessons.

"I don't have any money," the man told him, "but you can have those two horses out in the field."

Justin was not happy. Horses were expensive to keep. But the farmer had no money, so what could Justin do? With luck, he could sell the horses for enough money to feed his family. He sold the larger horse, but no one would buy the smaller one. So, Justin kept him. He named the horse *Figure*.

Morgans look great, whether standing still or moving. You can tell this horse is glad to be moving. Its head is high, and its ears are pricked forward.

RENT-A-HORSE TO LIVING LEGEND

Justin rented Figure to a neighbor. All day long, Figure would pull heavy trees and boulders from new farmland. Sometimes, Figure pulled huge logs the larger mill horses could not budge.

When he was not working, Figure also won races. Soon, everyone knew Figure was quite a horse! He became famous for his speed, strength, and small size. He was a fine-looking horse, too!

People brought mares to mate with Figure. No matter what kinds of mares had the foals, they all looked like Figure. They were fast and strong, too. People called these horses *Morgans*, after Justin Morgan's handsome, strong, little horse.

"Hey, Mom, wait up!" A mare waits eleven months to give birth to a foal (baby); humans wait nine. Yet, unlike human babies, foals can run only hours after they are born.

TOUGH AND PRETTY

All Morgans have a **conformation,** or build, like Figure. They are fourteen to fifteen **hands** high (about 5 feet, or 1.5 meters) at the **withers** — their shoulder area. They weigh 900 to 1,100 pounds (about 400 to 500 kilograms).

Morgans have faces that look intelligent. They have small, pointed ears and large eyes. They have dished faces, which means their faces curve in very slightly from their nostrils to their foreheads.

Morgans carry their heads high and always look proud. Note the slight dish between the nostrils and forehead.

PRETTY TOUGH

Morgans' backs are **close-coupled**. This means there is only a short distance between their withers and their croup (the slope to their tail on their backs). The result is that their muscles and bones are arranged to fit saddles well.

Morgans are lighter than the **draft horses** Figure beat in pulling contests. Their legs are shorter and thinner than those of draft horses. Yet, their rear muscles and feet are wider than those of other light horses. As a result, these good-looking horses are able to pull heavy loads.

Lucky rider! She has trained her Morgan to do a controlled trot. This allows her to sit while her Morgan moves faster than a walk.

MORGAN HORSE ANCESTORS

What breeds of horses were Figure's parents? It is a mystery. Some people say his ancestry included a mixture of Cob, Hackney, Andalusian, Quarter Horse, and Chickasaw.

Cobs and Hackneys are strong farm horses that gave Figure his strong legs. Andalusians are purebred horses from Spain that gave him his good looks. Quarter Horses are American racing horses, bred for speed. Chickasaws were originally bred by American Indians and gave Figure the strength to work hard and long.

It is not really important for anyone to solve the mystery, though. All Morgans are outstanding enough on their own four feet!

He is only a few days old, but centuries of breeding show in this Morgan foal's attitude.

"HERE IS THE STEED THAT SAVED THE DAY"

During the American Civil War, cavalries on both sides chose Morgans because they were calm in battle. A Union Army captain gave General Philip Sheridan a black Morgan. Sheridan named the horse *Rienzi*, for a town in Mississippi.

Once, by riding Rienzi many miles and calling out to his retreating troops, Sheridan gave his men the courage to turn around and fight their way to victory. Sheridan and Rienzi were admired for their spirit and endurance. Here is part of a stirring poem, written in their honor:

> *Be it said in letters both bold and bright:*
> *"Here is the steed that saved the day*
> *By carrying Sheridan into the fight,*
> *From Winchester — twenty miles away."*
>
> — Thomas Buchanan Read

At the Battle of Five Forks in April, 1865, General Sheridan jumped Rienzi over the Confederate defenses to help capture 150 soldiers.

KING OF THE WILD HORSES

Morgans are not fighting horses anymore. But some are famous as athletes and movie stars!

Rex was a glossy black Morgan movie star. In the 1920s and 1930s, Rex played a fierce stallion that "fought" wolves, cougars, other stallions, and mean movie characters.

Rex was very spirited in real life, too, creating a challenge for some of the actors and directors. The movie critics liked him, though. One said, "The beautiful animal is a great deal more intelligent than some human actors we have seen."

One of Rex's animal friends was Rin Tin Tin, the dog movie star. They were costars in many adventure movie series.

Black Dove, a glossy black Morgan that looks very much like Rex did, moves gently through a field at a special horse training center.

THE DO-IT-ALL HORSE

Morgans are best known for what they do — which is just about anything at all. They make brave police horses, noble parade horses, flashy harness horses, sporty polo ponies, and fine show horses in Western Riding and English Pleasure Riding classes.

When, over two hundred years ago, Justin Morgan went to collect his music-teaching pay, he had little idea he was going to get a horse instead. He had no idea at all he would get a horse that would bring him lasting fame.

For, as was the custom in New England in the 1700s, Figure's name was changed. He was renamed after his owner, Justin Morgan.

Morgans parade at a horse show. Imagine how amazed Justin Morgan would be today, to find a whole breed of beautiful horses named after him.

DIAGRAM AND SCALE OF A HORSE

Here's how to measure a horse with a show of hands.
This handsome Morgan has ideal conformation.

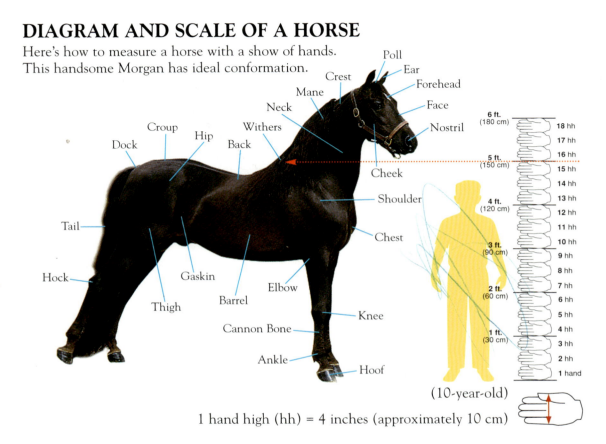

Poll
Ear
Forehead
Crest
Mane
Face
Neck
Nostril
Croup
Hip
Withers
Dock
Back
Cheek
Shoulder
Tail
Chest
Hock
Gaskin
Elbow
Thigh
Barrel
Knee
Cannon Bone
Ankle
Hoof

6 ft. (180 cm) 18 hh / 17 hh / 16 hh
5 ft. (150 cm) 15 hh / 14 hh / 13 hh
4 ft. (120 cm) 12 hh / 11 hh / 10 hh
3 ft. (90 cm)   9 hh / 8 hh / 7 hh
2 ft. (60 cm)   6 hh / 5 hh / 4 hh
1 ft. (30 cm)   3 hh / 2 hh / 1 hand

(10-year-old)

1 hand high (hh) = 4 inches (approximately 10 cm)

WHERE TO WRITE OR CALL FOR MORE INFORMATION

American Morgan Horse Association
3 Bostwick Road, P.O. Box 960
Shelbourne, VT 05482-0960
Phone: (802) 985-4944

MORE TO READ AND VIEW

Books (Nonfiction):   *The Complete Guides to Horses and Ponies* (series). Jackie Budd
                          (Gareth Stevens)
                          Great American Horses (series). Victor Gentle and Janet Perry
                          (Gareth Stevens)
                          Horses. Animal Families (series). Hans Dossenbach (Gareth Stevens)
                          I Can Be a Horse Trainer. Kathy Henderson (Childrens Press)
                          Magnificent Horses of the World (series). Tomáš Míček and
                          Dr. Hans-Jörg Schrenk (Gareth Stevens)
                          *Once Upon a Horse: A History of Horses and How They Shaped Our
                          Country*. Suzanne Jurmain (Lothrop, Lee & Shepard)
                          Wild Horses of the Red Desert. Glen Rounds (Holiday House)

Books (Fiction):   *Herds of Thunder, Manes of Gold*. Edited by B. Coville (Doubleday)
                       Justin Morgan Had a Horse. Marguerite Henry (Wilcox & Follett Co.)
                       Saddle Club (series). Bonnie Bryant (Gareth Stevens)
                       War Pony. Donald Emmet Worcester (Texas Christian University Press)

Videos (Fiction):   *The Black Stallion*. (MGM Home Video)
                        Justin Morgan Had a Horse. (Walt Disney)

WEB SITES

American Morgan Horse Association:
www.morganhorse.com

For interactive games:
www.haynet.net/kidstuff.html

For general horse information:
www.haynet.net
www.bcm.net
okstate.edu/breeds/horses

Due to the dynamic nature of the Internet, some web sites stay current longer than others. To find additional web sites, use a reliable search engine with one or more of the following keywords to help you locate information about horses: *Andalusians, Chickasaws, Cobs, equitation, Hackneys, Quarter Horses,* and *racing*.

GLOSSARY

You can find these words on the pages listed. Reading a word in a sentence helps you understand it even better.

bay — a dark, red-brown horse with black legs, mane, and tail 2

breed (n) — a group of horses that share the same features as a result of the careful selection of stallions and mares to produce foals 4, 14, 20

breed (v), **bred** — to choose a stallion and a mare with certain features to produce foals with similar features 4, 14

close-coupled (KLOS-cup-puld) — having a back with a short distance between the withers and the croup. Morgans' close-coupled backs hold a saddle well 12

conformation (KON-for-MAY-shun) — how a horse's body is built 10

draft horses — large, powerful breeds of horses used to pull heavy loads 12

hand — a unit about the width of a human hand used to measure horses and equal to 4 inches (10.2 cm) 10, 22

mate (v) — to join (animals) together to produce young; to breed a male and a female 4, 8

withers (WITH-erz) — the ridge between the shoulder bones of a horse. A horse's height is measured to its withers 10, 12, 22

INDEX